HerStory: Newham Asian Women's Project

She attended a focus group organised by NAWP to find out from service users what they felt should be the priorities going forward. Many voices were heard and they spoke about the need for housing, secured services for women and additional support. They understood resources were limited but said whatever could be done, should be done. Then one woman spoke and what she said focused the argument of the day on the interconnectedness of varied experiences. She said "…living through inflation meant that one week I buy the bread and the following week I buy the milk…" In need of support, fleeing domestic violence, struggling with economic poverty and being a woman in a society where you might not fall within the 'value for money' equation is a common story. Articulated by one woman in terms of bread and milk and it provided the context for the narrative for this book.

In 2012 Newham Asian Women's Project (NAWP) marks 25 years of service to women in the community. It remains a black feminist organisation providing gender-specific services. The project grew from the anti-racism movements of the early 1980s when women came together in safe space to debate and discuss their collective concerns around the discrimination they faced when they, and others from the communities from which they came, accessed public services. The need to challenge institutional racism that denied women equality came from experiences that could be framed within the context of political, social and economic exclusion. For South Asian women in particular, there was a need to mobilise in organised movement around the protection of their rights by articulating a vision around anti-racism and struggle against gender-based violence from within their communities., Within this context, NAWP started working under a framework of securing basic human rights for women and children.

Early debates and discussions drew from anti-colonial and independence movements as well as the movement of non-aligned countries. Combined, these struggles of resistance and assertion of black identity provided a framework for discussion around race in the context of a 'western democratic country'. NAWP's history is populated by the discourse on the intersection of race, gender and class as both definitive and constructive ideologies in the formation of political identity. Recognition of the interconnectedness of experiences around racism, classism, sexism and homophobia, among other struggles provided the ideological basis upon which NAWP could articulate its vision towards equality and rights.

Twenty-five years on it is important to re-visit political context and history, to remember how we formed and the politics of the time. Today many grassroots women's organisations are facing the struggle to survive harsh economic cuts. Some gender-specific organisations have adopted a gender-neutral stance. While the nature of political struggle changes with time, identity as organisation and movement must remain a constant. It is said many times that history must be re-visited when the struggle is the harshest. Documenting narratives on women's lives in this book through the words and imagery enables us to define who we are and where we stand.

Moving from historical context to the contemporary political space, identity remains critically at the centre of organisation and of movement. The economic cuts for instance are gendered placing women's services on the frontline.

The rationale for such severe cuts is found in the analysis of the interconnectedness of experience around race, gender and class. The world in which we live is often reconfigured by phrases such as 'bigger is better', 'efficiency savings' and 'value for money'. For women who need services, often the choices are stark and everyday decisions are made that affect the long term quality of life. It was not our intention to provide a comprehensive analysis of the state of affairs affecting women, however we find it necessary to draw attention to issues that continue to evidence the need for an organised effort to protect and promote the rights of women.

Addressing women's housing is at a critical stage. NAWP opened its first refuge in 1987 to provide emergency accommodation and support to women and children fleeing domestic violence. In 1996, NAWP opened a second stage refuge for women and children who were ready for semi-independent living. The purpose of this refuge was to enable women to get resettlement support to move-on to housing of their own. In 2001 NAWP expanded its refuge service to the London Borough of Haringey by taking over the direct management and frontline services of two women's refuges. In 2012 the women's refuge movement is facing a number of challenges. Value for Money (VfM) is used as a sector benchmark and many specialist services are being viewed as less competitive than mainstream counterparts because they operate in economies for scale. In addition to the economic imperative which determines models of 'efficiency' and 'effectiveness', to address homelessness there is a new standard for faster throughput. This means that length of stay in first stage emergency accommodation is shortened by as much as 6 to 9 months. With fewer affordable housing options available to women than two decades ago, women's housing is reaching crisis point.

NAWP became concerned about the changes to women's accommodation-based provision that was being driven predominantly by market factors. Early resettlement before women were emotionally, psychologically and economically ready to sustain housing of their own could result in repeat victimisation, engagement in further unhealthy relationships and failed housing jeopardising a woman's future potential to sustain housing. As affordable housing options are reduced, women at resettlement stage are also waiting longer to secure housing of their own affected by the economic downturn with their capacity to generate income impacted by the rising cost of child care, inflation, changes to the benefits system and fewer training and employment opportunities.

Looking back over 25 years, NAWP was set up to protect women against violence by providing refuge services. It went beyond accommodation to long-term sustainability offering training, therapeutic support, legal advice and information and other services. One of the most critical needs that women have today is access to safe and affordable housing. This book illustrates many journeys towards safety and freedom from violence. It is imperative that the policy framework graduate towards a gendered position on safeguarding women's needs with housing being critical among them.

For more than a decade, NAWP and a number of women's organisations had been calling on the government to abolish the two-year-rule for women with no recourse to public funds. There was ongoing concern that women with insecure immigration status, who have been subjected to gender-specific violence with no recourse to public funds, remain unprotected and have no access to social welfare assistance. In 2012, NAWP, along with sister organisations welcomed the Home Office concession allowing victims of domestic violence on spousal visas with no recourse

to public funds (NRPF) to access benefits and social housing while they apply for settlement under the 'domestic violence rule'. While many women benefit from the concession, NAWP provides services to many women with insecure immigration status who will not benefit from the exclusive and discriminatory safety net. Over 80 women per year with insecure immigration status access NAWP's legal advice and information service, more than half of whom are ineligible for support under the new concession. This is the local picture of one grassroots women's organisation. According to the data gathered by the No Recourse to Public Funds Campaign, nationally, 65% of women who accessed the Sojourner Project were ineligible for support leaving them in destitute situations which further jeopardised their wellbeing and safety. With limited options, women also had fewer choices to free themselves from violence. This meant that they were living in situations of violence for longer periods of time, risking health and life, and often made more vulnerable by circumstances of poverty, exclusion and isolation. There are further impacts. With recent cuts to legal aid, it is even more difficult for women to access appropriate immigration advice and related services which puts progress of cases in jeopardy coupled with a system that is already over-burdened.

It is obvious that women who suffer domestic and sexual violence require services regardless of their immigration status. NAWP supports the full recommendations to the Home Office of the NRPF Campaign to ensure all women have full access to benefits and services and that specialist support service are appropriately funded to deliver advice and assistance. NAWP also considers its arguments in the broader context of gendering sustainability where safeguarding of women, regardless of immigration status, who suffer gender-based violence are at the heart of policy. This not only makes good economic sense and lead to savings in the long-term but also protects women from further harm and addresses the problem of violence in society generally. NAWP produced this book to say that by supporting women, the whole of society benefits.

At a discussion with a group of women in one of NAWP's refuges in 2008, a woman said "…you have to remember, when I fled violence, I did not flee my culture, I fled the violence…" This quote articulated the need for specialist services at the time as offering community language support, culturally specific and with expertise to address gender-based violence. It reflected the view that cultures were not static and that the experience of violence is framed within the argument around women's unequal status to men and the persistence of patriarchy in governing relationship in both the public and private realm. The need for specialist services grows from specific needs including language and cultural understanding. Cultural specificity is important, however the context of violence affecting women's lives is found in patriarchy. The targeting of women's specialist services and the so-called mainstreaming of support to achieve efficiency by reducing the 'market' and the overhead associated with it is based upon a bias within policy about 'otherness'. By producing this book NAWP hopes to demonstrate the value of specialist services in alleviating violence against women and in addressing patriarchy. By expressing the stories, through words and images, we hope to convey the diverse experiences of women as culturally specific but affronting patriarchy in all its manifestations. 25 years on, it is still about the protection and promotion of women's rights with gender-specific violence as the core.

Newham Asian Women's Project

Dedication

This book is dedicated to all NAWP clients present and past who have served as an inspiration. Our special thanks to all those women who agreed to be photographed, shared their space with us and told us their stories.

Special Introduction by Meera Syal

I am proud to introduce this very special book depicting the lives and experiences of women who have interacted and connected with Newham Asian Women's Project. In the collection of photographs, you will find the journey to freedom from violence accompanied by the story about the objects they fled with that now decorate their rooms in the refuge and the special things that they hold close to their hearts. You will get a glimpse into dreams of the future putting to rest the reality of the painful past. You will come to understand how violence impacts women and children and what it takes to re-build life. Most importantly, collective women's survival spirits speak to us and the stories they tell will remain with you for some time.

Meera Syal
Patron, Newham Asian Women's Project

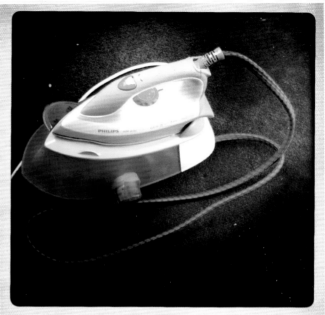

It is a badge, one of those that people design themselves. They take a photograph to a place where badges are made for the general public. In a matter of minutes a badge is made and it is personalised, belonging only to the person who wanted it made. This one contained a childhood memory with her brother. Next to it she keeps a key ring and a bangle. She marks her place in the world by these objects: a piece of memorabilia, a door imagined, and an ornament given and received, broken and whole, past and present combined.

She kept a card from the perpetrator. It contained the words 'wife', 'gorgeous' and 'sexy'. She also kept a postcard of the Taj Mahal - globally recognised as the monument to love. There were many memories of 'love' surrounding her life in the refuge. They had become passing moments, distant from what she now knew as she defined and re-defined her understanding and attachment to such words. She would still search for companionship with another. She would still want to discover love and share her life. She would not tolerate violence or harm of any kind. She was free.

Do not allow food bits to go in the drain. The drain is getting blocked.

Make sure all left over food is put in the bin before washing your plate. There should be no potato skin, rice etc in the sink / plug hole.

Thank & ...

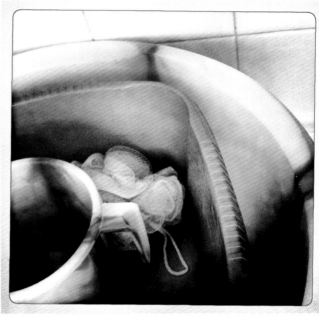

Moving with everything that belonged to her packed in boxes, the few suit cases she was able to claim and bin liners. One week later she was still unpacking, creating and defining her space, contemplating the path her life had taken and thinking about the journey ahead. Already talking about finding a job, she did not want to stay in the refuge long. Reconstructing, knowing that she had a life to live. In the kitchen she read the rules of communal living written on the wall. She knew them well. Applying the logic she had already learned from surviving violence, she knows where she is going.

I see water and feel its movement. A boat made of straw that will float for a moment. A basket woven in time that will stand as a monument to the home left behind. Not that of violence, but of a childhood place, when she was young, where water surrounded and its' stillness released a peace. Of straw and wicker, of movement and time, a life before violence is her most precious memory. She returns now from the safety of refuge to the way she used to think before she was married and when violence was subjected on her. To water, to movement, to a memory in time.

Standing with a cigarette in hand, the fence provides enclosure and in the room behind her, hair extensions are placed on the television. Women take on many roles in life and when they flee domestic violence, they leave some behind, transform others into the selves they often dreamed about being and strengthen parts of their identity marking themselves with the words freedom and independence.

Children live in refuges. They seek connection to childhood and also safety and solitude. A sense of space is important to them, creating and re-creating imagined worlds and filling them with play things resonates across refuges. They too re-build their lives from violence. They too flee from a perpetrator father. They too give context to the abuse they witness or suffer: at the top of a stair in another house, falling down, at the top of a stair in a refuge, finding a place to be.

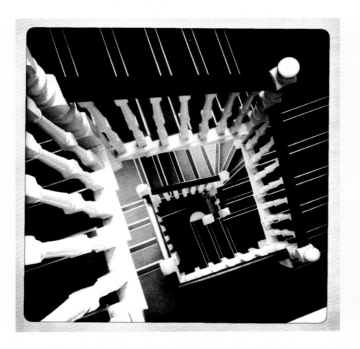

She saw butterflies as transformative beings mirroring her own life experiences. From the time of early childhood they were symbols of new beginnings, new worlds, and new ideas. Her life was changing as a photograph captured the moment. Leaves falling from pre-autumn trees paved the way towards the cycle of change that affected all life. A CCTV camera repeated imagery to express safety to those who would view it. Still, she carried with her the butterflies that reminded her of possibility. The refuge is safe house and haven, a place where things can stand still, only to move in directions seldom walked.

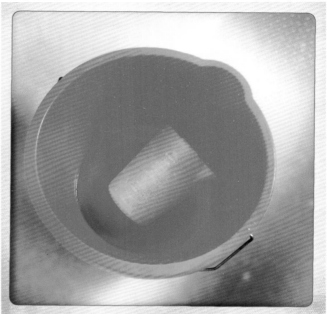

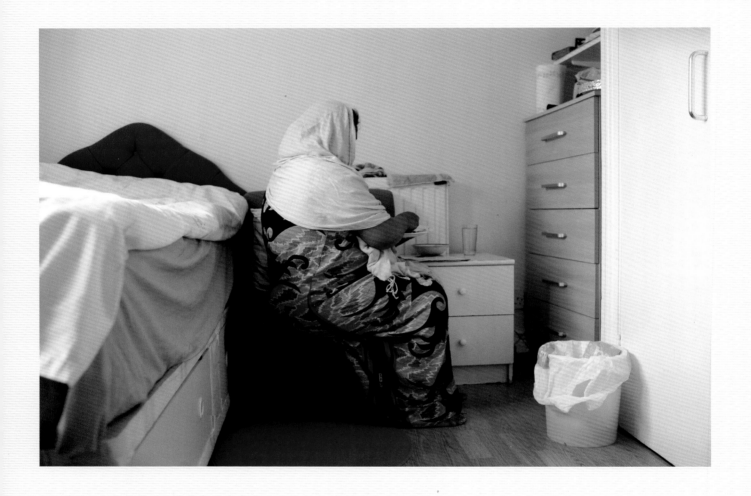

A refuge is shared space with communal areas for sitting and relaxing, watching television and for eating. A moment alone may only come in the 'bedspace' assigned to you. To the women who access refuges these spaces are so much more than filling a void. Sometimes they become the quiet spaces for a meal eaten in the company of one, and for time to reflect on the year approaching, completing Housing Benefit claims, getting a job, the ESOL class, to buy or not to buy a side table and the next move. While planning the move and calculating figures to make the numbers add for the rent, it is at all times a safe house.

There was a woman who collected bangles from other women. When asked why she did that she said they were reminders of the places she had visited and the women who inhabited them. On one of her journeys she came across another woman travelling to the place she had just left. She also collected bangles. When asked why she said that she did not like possessions that carried her but rather those that she could carry. The two women exchanged bangles and went on their way. It is a common scene, women arriving to a refuge with the bangles on their arms, sometimes with stories about who placed them there and where they came from, each similar to the other and different from the rest.

Why would anyone want to stay in a refuge? I know those who make decisions about how money is spent and write it down in their plans do not ask this question. I know some may think my experiences are not real. How could they be? Something so horrendous as abuse from a loved one can also linger in abstraction for those who do not know the women who flee. I know you want me to leave the refuge because I am not value for money. You think I should lock my trauma in a box by month three of my stay and just get on with it. Why would anyone want to stay in a refuge anyway?

Children flee domestic violence with their mothers. Some arrive at the refuge greeted by their own caseworker and given a child's induction. Some children are taken into custody and child contact is awarded to the mother for a few hours per week. Children are both victims and witnesses of domestic violence. Their lives are touched and damaged. They flee to safety. In the refuge many lives are re-constructed and many more relationships are re-built. With three children in custody, she is often running to meet them to have child contact and when she stops running, she is receiving support herself. When her support plan is met, she will start looking for a home for her children and herself.

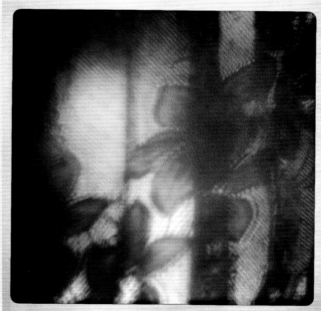

When she fled domestic violence, she took with her a photograph of her mother.

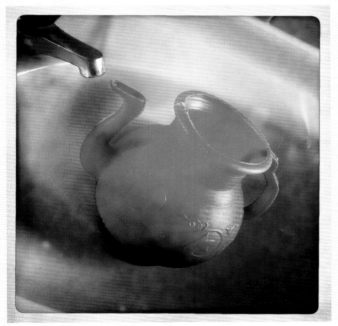

Boxes unpacked. It didn't take long. There were only two. A single suitcase is put away. A new life begins. It is free from violence and this expression cannot be said enough. She was pregnant when she arrived. Another baby born in the refuge implies the question 'why' and elicits the response 'to be free from violence'.

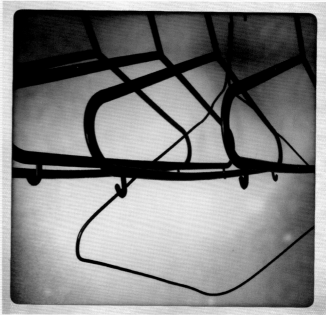

She is away. Life in the refuge is occupied by visits and activities. There are ESOL classes to subscribe to; registration at the GP, the benefits office, the housing team and the local job seekers office; and, visits to the library to access a PC. The business of ordering life and planning the move-on to the resettlement stage takes considerable time whilst at the refuge. In addition to the search for housing is the critical need for support after domestic violence.

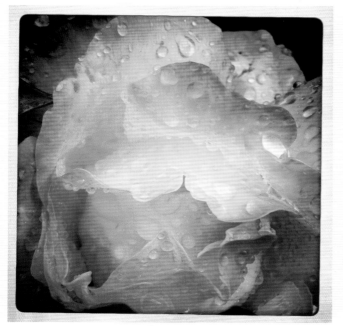

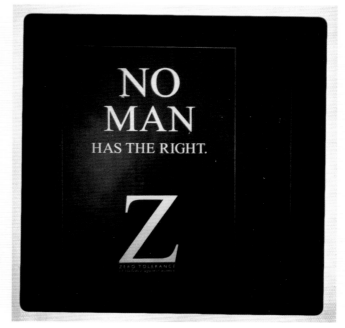

She reads poetry written long ago. Between verses she finds nature and connection. At the refuge poetry offers her language and her books give her peace of mind. In her thoughts she writes about her experiences and reflects on the moment that brought her to safety. Her language is fluid, she writes about her dress, her dress is hanging away from her, she understands its place in her life and she can only express it in poetry.

On the wall, the attendance records of the children in the refuge. They all get A+. A child writes 'I love you' to her mother, leaving it on the bathroom wall for her to see when she bathes that morning. It will be a wonderful sight. She needs to see those words that day. The house rules complete the collage of words and messages to those who reside within the walls and under the roof of the safe house. Life goes on after domestic violence. The refuge provides the bricks and mortar, the women and children create community and belonging, and the work begins again.

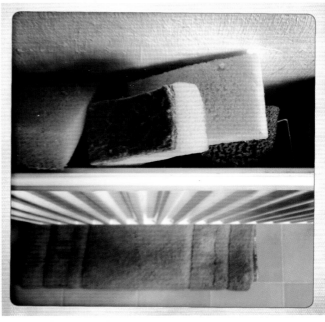

She has a neat stack of books on her dressing room table. She reads frequently to keep her mind occupied. She travels when she reads. She imagines when she travels. She creates when she imagines. She probably had a similar stack of books when she was in school. Now she has fled domestic violence. She finds meaning in her books that was perhaps not there before. Reality has been stirred and thrown off the axis but she has her books and her opportunities are reborn.

Contained and sealed, the plastic boxes from her mother for possessions for safekeeping when she fled. A panic alarm for safety if this should ever be in jeopardy again. A book given to her child with the words 'I wish'. Her understanding of the word 'safety' is both personalised and externalised giving her history and future, she is linked to environment, culture and identity and free from violence. Her portrait of herself is completing and ever changing. She has fled.

Hair: designing it, shaping it, cutting it. That was her 'thing'. A calendar: mapping and planning, picking dates for milestones to fall and turning the page when it is all done. That was her task. Shoes: worn and comfortable, located specifically in the room, ready to go. That was the reminder that the refuge was but a stepping stone. She was trained, she sought employment, she wanted movement, she desired change, she wanted life.

A wedding day sari is both a memory of happiness and a reason for suffering. She puts it on now to remember a moment in time and to remind herself of the journey to freedom she took. Her child's embraces comfort her, showing her the imprints in the grass of the steps they have taken together. She likes the design, the colour and the feeling of silk. She likes that she can wear it as she pleases and take it off and put it away for another occasion.

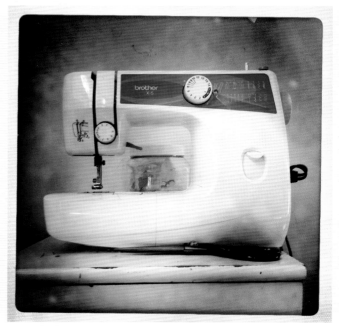

A rickshaw from somewhere else occupies space in this room. A sewing machine bought elsewhere takes up another corner. These are belongings that came from another house where they were placed in a room with other things. It was all she could carry with her: a tool for making clothes and a memory from a country she left long ago. These things give her identity in which she seeks comfort. It cannot be taken from her, not by violence and not by fleeing. She is free, she is free now.

Newham Asian Women's Project

Working for Woman, Working against Violence

Newham Asian Women's Project
661 Barking Road
Plaistow
London
E13 9EX

T: 020 8472 0528
W: www.nawp.org
E: info@nawp.org

Concept and Project Managed by Anjum Mouj
Written by Baljit Banga
Edited by Kaveri Sharma
Photographed by Vicki Couchman:
T: 07957 226 911
W: vickicouchman.com
E: vicki@vickicouchman.com

Printed by Printhouse Corporation:
T: 020 8963 0123
W: printhouse.co.uk